الصدق مع الله

Being Truthful
with
Allāh

Shaykh 'Abdur-Razzāq Ibn 'Abdul-Muhsin al-'Abbād al-Badr

ISBN: 978-1-9442-4133-9

First Edition: Muharram1437 A.H. /October 2015 C.E.

Cover Design: Abū Sulaymān Muhammad 'Abdul-Azim Ibn Joshua Baker

Translation by Abū 'Abdillah Khalīl 'Abdur Razzāq

Revision of translation by Rāha Batts

Editing by Abdullah Bin Ali as-Somali

Typesetting & formatting by Abū Sulaymān Muhammad 'Abdul-'Azim Ibn Joshua Baker

Printing: Ohio Printing

Subject: Akhlāq

Website: www.maktabatulirshad.com
E-mail: info@maktabatulirshad.com

BRIEF BIOGRAPHY OF THE AUTHOR

His name: Shaykh 'Abdur-Razzāq Ibn 'Abdul-Muhsin al-'Abbād al-Badr.

He is the son of the *'Allāmah* and *Muhaddith* of Medina Shaykh 'Abdul-Muhsin al 'Abbād al-Badr.

Birth: He was born on the 22nd day of *Dhul-Qa'dah* in the year 1382 AH in az-Zal'fi, Kingdom of Saudi Arabia. He currently resides in Medina.

Current Occupation: He is a member of the teaching staff at the Islāmic University of Medina.

Scholastic Certifications: Doctorate in *'Aqīdah*.

The Shaykh has authored books, researches, as well as numerous explanations in different sciences. Among them are:

1. *Fiqh of Supplications & adh-Kār.*

2. *Hajj & Refinement of the Souls.*

3. Explanation of the book, *Exemplary Principles*, by Shaykh Ibn 'Uthaymīn (رَحِمَهُٱللَّه).

4. Explanation of the book, *The Principles of Names & Attributes*, authored by Shaykh-ul-Islām Ibn al-Qayyim (رَحِمَهُٱللَّه).

5. Explanation of the book, *Good Words*, authored by Shaykh-ul-Islām Ibn al-Qayyim (رَحِمَهُٱللَّه).

6. Explanation of the book, *al-Aqīdah at-Tahāwiyyah*.

7. Explanation of the book, *Fusūl: Biography of the Messenger*, by Ibn Kathīr (رَحِمَهُٱللَّه).

8. A full explanation of the book, *al-Adab-ul-Mufrad*, authored by Imam Bukhārī (رَحِمَهُٱللَّه).

From the most distinguished scholars whom he has taken and acquired knowledge from are:

1. His father the *'Allāmah* Shaykh 'Abdul-Muhsin al-Badr (حفظه الله).

2. The *'Allāmah* Shaykh Ibn Bāz (رَحِمَهُٱللَّه).

3. The *'Allāmah* Shaykh Muhammad Ibn Sālih al-'Uthaymīn (رَحِمَهُٱللَّه).

4. Shaykh 'Ali Ibn Nāsir al-Faqīhi (حفظه الله).

ARABIC SYMBOL TABLE

Arabic Symbols & their meanings

حفظه الله	May Allāh preserve him
رَضِىَاللَّهُعَنْهُ	(i.e. a male companion of the Prophet Muhammad)
سُبْحَانَهُوَتَعَالَى	Glorified & Exalted is Allāh
عَزَّوَجَلَّ	(Allāh) the Mighty & Sublime
تَبَارَكَوَتَعَالَى	(Allāh) the Blessed & Exalted
جَلَّوَعَلَا	(Allāh) the Sublime & Exalted
عَلَيْهِالصَّلَاةُوَالسَّلَامُ	May Allāh send Blessings & Safety upon him (i.e. a Prophet or Messenger)
صَلَّىاللَّهُعَلَيْهِوَعَلَىآلِهِوَسَلَّمَ	May Allāh send Blessings & Safety upon him and his family (i.e. Du'ā send mentioned the Prophet Muhammad)
رَحَمَهُاللَّهُ	May Allāh have mercy upon him
رَضِىَاللَّهُعَنْهُمْ	May Allāh be pleased with them (i.e. Du'ā made for the Companions of the Prophet Muhammad)
جَلَّجَلَالُهُ	(Allāh) His Majesty is Exalted
رَضِىَاللَّهُعَنْهَا	May Allāh be pleased with her (i.e. a female companion of the Prophet Muhammad)

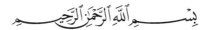

All praise is due to Allāh, the Lord of all that exists. I bear witness that none deserves to be worshipped in truth except Allāh alone with no partners, and I bear witness that Muhammad is His slave and Messenger (may Allāh send *Salāh*[1] and peace upon him, his family, and his companions all-together).

As for what follows:

Verily, the subject matter of this treatise is extremely important and gatherings should be held to discuss and contemplate that which it contains due to its magnitude, importance and urgent need. The happiness of the servant in his worldly life and Hereafter is dependent upon its actualization. There is no safety nor happiness for him in this worldly life or the Hereafter unless he is from its people. Whoever

---

[1] Shaykh Muhammad ibn Sālih al-'Uthaymīn (رحمه الله) said in his explanation to his book, *Usūl Min 'Ilm Usūl*: " Abū al-'Āliyyah (رحمه الله) said: "Allāh's *Salāh* upon His slave is Allāh's praise for him in the highest gathering." (Dār ibn al-Jawzi Edition, 21).

studies the Book of Allāh (عَزَّوَجَلَّ) and the Sunnah of His noble Prophet (صَلَّى ٱللَّهُ عَلَيْهِ وَسَلَّمَ) knows its great and extensive importance as well as its loftiness: Truthfulness is a lofty, great rank from the various ranks of those who advance to Allāh (تَبَارَكَ وَتَعَالَى). Every action of the heart returns to it just as every corruption that occurs in the heart returns exclusively to its opposite, which is lying. The source of all rectification for the outward or inner condition of a man lies in truthfulness and the source of every corruption in the outward, and inward appearance of man is lying; thus good and corruption return to these two sources.

Allāh (تَبَارَكَ وَتَعَالَى) has made this world a life of calamity and trial so that the truthful distinguishes himself from the liar. Allāh (تَبَارَكَ وَتَعَالَى) said:

﴿ الٓمٓ ۝ أَحَسِبَ ٱلنَّاسُ أَن يُتْرَكُوٓاْ أَن يَقُولُوٓاْ ءَامَنَّا وَهُمْ لَا يُفْتَنُونَ ۝ وَلَقَدْ فَتَنَّا ٱلَّذِينَ مِن قَبْلِهِمْ فَلَيَعْلَمَنَّ ٱللَّهُ ٱلَّذِينَ صَدَقُواْ وَلَيَعْلَمَنَّ ٱلْكَٰذِبِينَ ۝ ﴾

"Alif-Lām-Mīm. Do people think that they will be left alone because they say: "We believe," and will not be tested. And We indeed tested those who were before them. And Allāh will certainly make (it) known (the truth of) those who are true, and will certainly make (it) known (the falsehood of) those who are liars. (Although Allāh knows all that before putting them to test)." [Sūrah al-Ankabut 29:1-3]

Meaning: This life is a field for examination and an abode of trials. Allāh has tested those who came before us from the various nations in this life: **"And We indeed tested those who were before them,"** meaning, He (جَلَّوَعَلَا) tested and examined them with what will distinguish the people of truth from the people of falsehood by way of it. And like them, this nation itself is subjected to being tested.

The meaning of Allāh's statement: **"And Allāh will certainly make it known…,"** is that He will see it, because what is intended here by knowledge (**"make it known"**) is vision; meaning, He will know it with the knowledge of sight and occurrence for this thing since Allāh's knowledge of His servants' actions is eternal knowledge that preceded the fulfillment of the actions and knowledge of them after their occurrence — this is what is meant here and it is what reward and punishment will result from.

The testing in this life through which the truthful is distinguished from the liar returns to two matters:

1. Being tested with blameworthy doubts in both knowledge and belief.

2. Being tested with blameworthy desires in one's wishes and actions.

So whomever Allāh (جَلَّوَعَلَا) grants success to in being safe from doubts when they appear through what Allāh has given him of the correct and firm belief, truthfulness and a strong relationship with Him (تَبَارَكَوَتَعَالَ), as well his turning back to Him; verily, he will succeed in this test and fare well.

Likewise, if callers to desires come to him and he thus avoids them and takes refuge by way of obedience and drawing close to Allāh, seeking safety from them and running away from their trails and pathways; he will similarly prosper with success from Allāh (عَزَّوَجَلَّ) in this test.

As for he—and refuge is sought by Allah-- who is swept away by doubts or destroyed by his desires; then this is the indications and signs of him not having truthfulness with Allāh or having weakness in his truthfulness—and Allāh's refuge is sought. By way of this, the people are distinguished and divided into two groups:

• The group of truthfulness.

• The group of falsehood.

The one sincere to himself aspires to constrict doubtful matters under the direction of the legislation and takes hold of them by way of its limitations and guidelines to be secure from destruction and succeed in this great test—and success is in the Hand of Allāh (تَبَارَكَ وَتَعَالَى) alone with no partners. Allāh (عَزَّوَجَلَّ) has said:

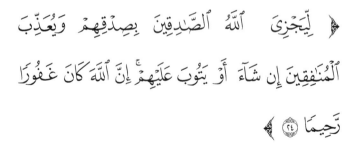

"That Allāh may reward the men of truth for their truth, and punish the hypocrites if He

will or accept their repentance by turning to them in mercy. Verily, Allāh is Oft-Forgiving, Most Merciful." [*Sūrah al-Ahzāb* 33:24]

Since truthfulness has this high standing and this lofty degree, the texts are many **which incite** towards it and awaken a desire for it along with clarifying its virtue and the loftiness of its degree. There is no safety for the servant except by way of it. **And from these (texts)** is the statement of Allāh:

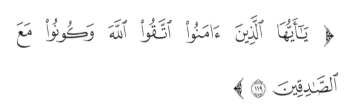

"O you who believe! Be afraid of Allāh, and be with those who are true (in words and deeds)." [*Sūrah at-Tawbah* 9:119]

This is a command for the servants to be with the truthful, i.e., with the people of truthfulness. And the Muslim is not considered to be with them unless he adorns himself with their embellishment and is characterized by their description. By way of that he will be from amongst them. This divine order came after the mention of Allāh accepting the repentance of the three who were left behind in the expedition of Tabūk. Their salvation did not materialize except on the account of their truthfulness with Allāh (سُبْحَانَهُوَتَعَالَ) and with His Messenger (صَلَّأَللَّهُعَلَيْهِوَسَلَّمَ) and their avoidance of and remaining distant from lying. Truthfulness is a safeguard, strength, and tranquility; whereas lying is an abyss, doubt, and defeat.

There is a story of the group of three individuals in a time before us whom a boulder had closed upon them in the cave. It is narrated in the two Sahīhs (al-Bukhārī and Muslim) and other than them from the Hadīth of Ibn 'Umar, Abū Hurayrah, Anas (رَضِّأَللَّهُعَنْهُمْ), and other than them. In the narration found in Sahīh al-Bukhārī from the Hadīth of Ibn 'Umar (رَضِّأَللَّهُعَنْهُمَا), when the boulder closed on these three, some of them said to the others:

إِنَّهُ وَ اللهِ يَا هَؤُلَاءِ، لَا يُنْجِيكُمْ إِلَّا الصِّدْقُ ،

فَلْيَدْعُ كُلُّ رَجُلٍ مِنْكُمْ بِمَا يَعْلَمُ أَنَّهُ قَدْ صَدَقَ

فِيهِ.

"By Allāh! Nothing will save you except truthfulness. Therefore, let every man from

you call upon Allāh with what he knows he was truthful concerning."[2]

Pay attention to this! Not every outward action is considered truthfulness with Allāh (تَبَارَكَوَتَعَالَى); rather, truthfulness with Allāh is solely a matter that returns to the heart and the interior of a person, as well as what the person intends and wishes to achieve with this action. For this reason, when every single one of them was seeking to use their righteous actions as a means to draw close to Allāh one of them sought to use his righteousness to his parents, the other did so by way of his abstinence from fornication after having had a strong desire and then the ability to actually commit it, the third did so by way of his fulfilling the right of his laborer, giving him his rate and an increase. While seeking [to use their deeds as] a means to Allāh (تَبَارَكَوَتَعَالَى), they all said:

إِنْ كُنْتَ تَعْلَمُ أَنِّي فَعَلْتُ ذَلِكَ ابْتِغَاءَ وَجْهِكَ

فَافْرُجْ عَنَّا فُرْجَةً.

---

[2] Saḥīḥ al-Bukhārī #3465

"If you know that I did this seeking your face (i.e., for your sake), open for us a gap."[3]

Truthfulness is a safe haven for the servant from the trials of this life, its hardships, horrors, and calamities; it is also protection for him on the day that he will stand before Allāh (تَبَارَكَوَتَعَالَى).

Allāh (عَزَّوَجَلَّ) said:

﴿ هَذَا يَوْمُ يَنفَعُ ٱلصَّٰدِقِينَ صِدْقُهُمْ لَهُمْ جَنَّٰتٌ تَجْرِى مِن تَحْتِهَا ٱلْأَنْهَٰرُ خَٰلِدِينَ فِيهَآ أَبَدًا رَّضِىَ ٱللَّهُ عَنْهُمْ وَرَضُواْ عَنْهُ ذَٰلِكَ ٱلْفَوْزُ ٱلْعَظِيمُ ۝ ﴾

"This is a Day on which the truthful will profit from their truth: theirs are Gardens under which rivers flow (in Paradise) – they shall abide therein forever. Allāh is pleased with them and they with Him. That is a great success (Paradise)." [*Sūrah al-Mā'idah* 5:119]

Therefore, entrance into the Gardens and success with the attainment of Allāh's pleasure (سُبْحَانَهُوَتَعَالَى) only

---

[3] Sahīh al-Bukhārī #3465

comes about by way of having truthfulness with Him
(عَزَّوَجَلَّ). Regarding this meaning Allāh (جَلَّوَعَلَا) said:

**"And when the matter (preparation for *Jihād*)
is resolved on, then if they had been true to
Allāh, it would have been better for them."**
[*Sūrah Muhammad* 47:21]

Prosperity, salvation, benevolence, happiness, and
success are tied to having truthfulness with Allāh
(عَزَّوَجَلَّ). The texts regarding this meaning are many, and
every one of them emphasizes the magnitude of
truthfulness as well as the extreme need for having
concern and attaching importance to it. There is no
salvation nor success for the servant in this life nor the
Hereafter except by way of it.

From what indicates the great station of truthfulness
is that it is a pillar which the *Tawhīd* of Allāh[4] (عَزَّوَجَلَّ) is

---

[4] **Translator's notes:** Tawhīd is singling out Allāh alone with what
is specific to Him. Its parts are three:

established upon; for verily, the *Tawhīd* of Allāh (جَلَّوَعَلَا)
is established upon two great pillars and two solid
foundations:

• Truthfulness.

• Sincerity.

Just as Ibn al-Qayyim (رَحِمَهُٱللَّه)said in his poem '*an-Nuniyyah*':

وَ الـصِّـدْقُ وَ الْإِخْـلَاصُ رُكْـنَـا ذَلِكَ

الـتَّـوْحِـيـدِكَـالرُّكْـنَـيْنِ لِلْبُنْيَانِ

**"And truthfulness and sincerity are two pillars
of that (*Tawhīd*) *** Just like two pillars for a
building structure."[5]**

So, the *Tawhīd* of Allāh is established upon sincerity
and truthfulness. The difference between the two of

_____

• Tawhīd *ar-Rubūbiyyah* (Singling Allāh out alone in His
Lordship).
• Tawhīd *al-Ulūhiyyah* or Tawhīd *al-'Ibādah* (Singling Allāh out
with worship).
• Tawhīd *al-Asmā' was Sifāt* (Singling Allāh out with His Names
and Attributes). This definition can be found in Shaykh
Muhammad ibn Salih al-'Uthaymin's explanation of *Kitab Tawhid*.
[5] *an-Nuniyyah* (Ibn al-Qayyim, 219)

them is that sincerity is the *Tawhīd* of the intended goal for the One, Who is worshipped, Who is resorted to so that none is made a partner with Him in worship and He alone is singled out with worship. As for truthfulness, it is the *Tawhīd* of one's wish and request; and that is with the assembly of the heart, ambition, and resolve for the fulfillment of worship — completing and fulfilling it — and not busying the heart with other than it. So, sincerity is the act of worship that is intended, and truthfulness is the *Tawhīd* of one's wish. Concerning this, Ibn al-Qayyim (رَحِمَهُ ٱللَّهُ) said in his book, *an-Nūniyyah*:

فَلِـوَاحِدٍ كُـنْ وَاحِدًا فِي وَاحِدِ

أَعْنِي سَبِيلَ الْـحَقِّ وَ الْإِيـمَـان

"So for one, be a monotheist, concerning one * I mean the path of truth and *Imān*."** [6]

Imān and the focus of salvation are established upon these three pillars:

---

[6] *an-Nuniyyah* of Ibnul (Ibn al-Qayyim: Page, 219)

1. Sincerity: His statement, *"so for one,"* means, sincerely, i.e., do not take any partners with Him.

2. Truthfulness: His statement, *"one, be a monotheist"* means, be truthful with your determination, resolve, diligence, and endeavor.

3. Compliance: His statement, "concerning one," means, following the path of truth and *Imān*.

Therefore, by way of these three matters, the servant is granted happiness, prosperity, success, and safety in this life as well as the Hereafter. For this reason, truthfulness and sincerity are joined. Look at their connection in the statement of Allāh (عَزَّوَجَلَّ):

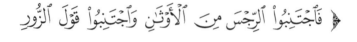

"So shun the abomination (worshipping) of idol, and shun lying speech (false statements)"
[*Sūrah al-Hajj* 22:30]

Shunning the worship of idols is by way of sincerity to Allāh and the shunning of lying speech is by way of truthfulness. With these two is safety for the servant and success in his worldly life as well as his Hereafter.

Sincerity and truthfulness are two conditions for the acceptance of the statement of *Tawhīd* (*Lā ilāha illa Allāh* (None deserves to be worshipped in truth except Allāh). There occurs in the Sahīh of al-Bukhārī from the *Hadīth* of Abū Hurayrah (رَضِيَاللهُعَنهُ) that he said:

قِيـلَ: يَا رَسُولَ اللهِ! مَنْ أَسْعَدَ النَّاسِ بِشِفَاعَتِكَ يَوْمَ الْقِيَامَةِ؟ قَالَ رَسُولُ اللهِ صَلَّى اللهُ عَلَيْهِ وَ سَلَّمَ :((لَقَدْ ظَنَنْتُ يَا أَبَا هُرَيْرَةَ، أَنْ لَا يَسْأَلَنِي عَنْ هَذَا الْحَدِيثِ أَحَدٌ أَوَّلُ مِنْكَ ، لِمَا رَأَيْتُ مِنْ حِرْصِكَ عَلَى الْحَدِيثِ ، أَسْعَدُ النَّاسِ بِشَفَاعَتِي يَوْمَ الْقِيَامَةِ، مَنْ قَالَ : لَا إِلَهَ إِلَّا اللهُ ، خَالِصًا مِنْ قَلْبِهِ ، أَوْ نَفْسِهِ)) .

"It was said: 'O Messenger of Allāh! Who will be the happiest person who will gain your intercession on the Day of Resurrection?' The Messenger of Allāh said: 'O Abū Hurayrah! I

have thought that none would ask me about it before you because of what I have seen from your endeavor for *Hadīth*. The happiest person who will have my intercession on the Day of Resurrection will be the one who said: *Lā ilāha illa Allāh* (None deserves to be worshipped in truth except Allāh) sincerely from his heart."[7]

Also in the two Sahīhs of al-Bukhārī and Muslim on the authority of Anas ibn Mālik (رَضِىَٱللَّهُعَنْهُ):

أَنَّ النَّبِيَّ صَلَّى اللهُ عَلَيْهِ وَ سَلَّمَ وَ مُعَاذَ رَضِيَ
اللهُ عَنْهُ رَدِيفُهُ عَلَى الرَّحلِ ، قَالَ : يَا مُعَاذُ ابْنَ
جَبَلٍ ، قَالَ : لَبَّيْكَ يَا رَسُولَ اللهِ وَ سَعَيْكَ ، قَالَ
: يَا مُعَاذُ ، قَالَ لَبَّيْكَ يَا رَسُولَ اللهِ وَ سَعَيْكَ –
ثَلَاثًا – ، قَالَ : مَا مِنْ أَحَدٍ يَشْهَدُ أَنْ لَا إِلَهَ إِلَّا اللهُ
، وَ أَنَّ مُحَمَّدًا رَسُولُ اللهِ ، صِدْقًا مِنْ قَلْبِهِ ، إِلَّا
حَرَّمَهُ اللهُ عَلَى النَّارِ . قَالَ: يَا رَسُولَ اللهِ ، أَفَلَا

---

[7] *Sahīh al-Bukhārī* (99, 6570)

أُخْبِرُ بِهِ النَّاسَ فَيَسْتَبْشِرُوا؟ قَالَ: إِذًا يَتَّكِلُوا،

وَ أَخْبَرَ بِهَا مُعَاذٌ رَضِيَ اللهُ عَنْهُ عِنْدَ مَوْتِهِ

تَأَثُّمًا.

Mu'ādh bin Jabal was riding on the beast with the Prophet (ﷺ) when he (ﷺ) said to him, "'O Mu'ādh!' Mu'ādh replied, 'Here I am responding to you, and at your pleasure, O Messenger of Allāh.' He (ﷺ) again called out, 'O Mu'ādh.' He (again) replied, 'Here I am responding your call, and at your pleasure.' He (Messenger of Allāh) addressed him (again), 'O Mu'ādh!' He replied, 'Here I am responding to you, and at your pleasure, O Messenger of Allāh.' Upon this he (the Prophet (ﷺ)) said, 'If anyone testifies sincerely that there is none who deserves to be worshipped in truth except Allāh, and Muhammad is His slave and Messenger, truly from his heart, Allāh will safeguard him from Hell.' He (Mu'ādh) said, 'O Messenger of Allāh, shall I not then inform people of it, so that they may have glad tidings.' He (ﷺ) said: 'They will rely on it alone (and thus give up good acts altogether).' Mu'ādh (رضي الله عنه) disclosed this Hadīth at the time of his death to avoid sinning for concealing it."[8]

So sincerity was imposed as a condition in the first *Hadīth* and truthfulness as a condition in the second *Hadīth*; therefore, whoever is not sincere regarding *Lā ilāha illa Allāh* is a *Mushrik* (one who associates partners with Allāh) and whoever is not truthful regarding this statement is a hypocrite as Allāh (سبحانه وتعالى) has stated:

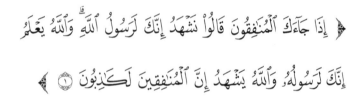

"When the hypocrites come to you (O Muhammad), they say: "We bear witness that you are indeed the Messenger of Allāh." Allāh knows that you are indeed His Messenger, and Allāh bears witness that the hypocrites are liars." [*Sūrah al-Munafiqun* 63:1]

---

[8] *Sahīh al-Bukhārī* (128) and this is his wording, *Sahīh Muslim* (32)

And it is binding that the statement "*Lā ilāha illa Allāh*"
by the servant: "*La Ilāha Illā Allāh* (None deserves to be
worshipped in truth except Allāh)" is binding that it
emanates from a truthful heart so that Allāh will accept
it from him and so that he can truly and honestly be
from its people. If he, however, did not say it from a
truthful heart but merely uttered it with his tongue
alone, he will not benefit from it and be considered
from its people.

It has come on the authority of Abū Hurayrah and Abū
Sa'īd (رَضِيَاللهُعَنْهُمَا) that they said:

إِذَا قَالَ الْعَبْدُ : لَا إِلَـهَ إِلَّا اللهُ، وَاللهُ أَكْبَرُ، صَدَّقَهُ رَبُّهُ

، قَالَ : صَدَقَ عَبْدِي، لَا إِلَـهَ إِلَّا أَنَا، وَ أَنَا أَكْبَرُ،

وَ إِذَا قَالَ : لَا إِلَـهَ إِلَّا اللهُ وَحْدَهُ، صَدَّقَهُ رَبُّهُ ، قَالَ :

صَدَقَ عَـبْدِي، لَا إِلَـهَ إِلَّا أَنَا وَحْـدِي ، وَ إِذَا قَـالَ : لَا

إِلَـهَ إِلَّا اللهُ لَا شَـرِيكَ لَهُ ، صَدَّقَهُ رَبُّهُ ، قَالَ : صَدَقَ

عَـبْدِي، لَا إِلَـهَ إِلَّا أَنَا لَا شَـرِيكَ لِي، وَ إِذَا قَالَ : لَا

إِلَـهَ إِلَّا اللهُ لَـهُ الْمُـلْكُ وَلَهُ الْحَـمْدُ، صَـدَّقَهُ رَبُّهُ،

قَالَ : صَدَقَ عَبْدِي ، لَا إِلَهَ إِلَّا أَنَا ، وَلِيَ الْمُلْكُ وَ

لِيَ الْحَمْدُ ، صَدَّقَهُ رَبُّهُ ، قَالَ : صَدَقَ عَبْدِي ، لَا

إِلَهَ إِلَّا أَنَا ، لِيَ الْمُلْكُ وَلِي الْحَمْدُ ، وَ إِذَا قَالَ :

لَا إِلَهَ إِلَّا اللهُ ، لَا حَوْلَ وَ لَا قُوَّةَ إِلَّا بِاللهِ ، صَدَّقَهُ

رَبُّهُ ، وَ قَالَ : صَدَقَ عَبْدِي ، لَا إِلَهَ إِلَّا أَنَا ، وَ لَا

حَوْلَ قُوَّةَ إِلَّا بِي .

"If a person says: 'La Ilāha Illā Allāhu wa Allāhu Akbar (None has the right to be worshipped in truth except Allāh and Allāh is the Most Great),' Allāh says: 'My slave has spoken the truth; there is none who has the right to be worshipped in truth except Me, and I am the Most Great.' If a person says: 'Lā ilāha illa Allāh wahdah (There is none who has the right to be worshipped in truth except Allāh alone),' Allāh says: 'My slave has spoken the truth; there is none worthy of worship except I, alone.' If he says, Lā ilāha illa Allāhu la sharīka lah (There is none who has the right to be worshipped in truth except Allāh with no partner),' Allāh says: 'My slave has spoken the truth; there is none who has the right to be worshipped in truth except Me, with no partner.' If he says: '*Lā ilāha illa Allāh, lahul mulku wa lahul hamd* (There is none who has the right to be worshipped in truth except Allāh, all dominion is His, and all praise is due to Him),' Allāh says: 'My slave has spoken the truth; there is none who has the right to be worshipped in truth except Me, all dominion is Mine and all praise is due to Me.' If he says: '*Lā ilāha illa Allāh, la hawla wa la quwwata illa billah* (There is none who deserves to be worshipped in truth except Allāh, and there is no power and no strength except with Allāh),' Allāh says: 'My slave has spoken the truth; there is none worthy of worship except Me, and there is no power and no strength except with Me."[9]

Contemplate all of this with the repetition of the statement of *Tawhīd: Lā ilāha illa Allāh*.

---

[9] Reported by at-Tirmidhī in his *'al-'Jāmi'* (3430), Ibn Mājah in his *Sunan* (3794), and Ibn Hibān in his *Sahīh* (851) and this is his wording.

In this great *Hadīth,* the statement of Allāh is repeated: "My slave has spoken the truth." Halt at His statement: "My slave," Verily, this servitude—that is adjoined to Allāh (عَزَّوَجَلَّ) which necessitates nobility, honor, virtue, and the bestowal of favor—will only be attained by those who are truthful in their statement of *Lā ilāha illa Allāh.* However, whoever says it by way of his tongue without it being truthful from his heart, this will not benefit him. Rather, with the lack of truthfulness in his statement—if he dies upon it—he will be from the people of the lowest depths of the Fire.

It is binding to have truthfulness with the statement of *Lā ilāha illa Allāh* and to regard it; the people are divided into two groups: a lying disbeliever and a truthful believer.

Allāh says:

﴿ ۞ فَمَنْ أَظْلَمُ مِمَّن كَذَبَ عَلَى ٱللَّهِ وَكَذَّبَ بِٱلصِّدْقِ إِذْ جَآءَهُۥٓ أَلَيْسَ فِي جَهَنَّمَ مَثْوًى لِّلْكَٰفِرِينَ ۞ وَٱلَّذِى جَآءَ بِٱلصِّدْقِ وَصَدَّقَ بِهِۦٓ

أُوْلَٰٓئِكَ هُمُ ٱلْمُتَّقُونَ ۝ لَهُم مَّا يَشَآءُونَ عِندَ

رَبِّهِمْ ذَٰلِكَ جَزَآءُ ٱلْمُحْسِنِينَ ۝ ﴾

"Then, who does more wrong than one who utters a lie against Allāh, and denies the truth when it comes to him! Is there not in Hell an abode for the disbelievers? And he (Muhammad (ﷺ)) who has brought the truth and (those who) believed therein, those are al-Muttaqūn (the pious). They shall have all that they will desire with their Lord. That is the reward of Muhsinūn (good-doers)." [*Sūrah az-Zumar* 39:32-34]

So, Allāh (عَزَّوَجَلَّ) mentioned that the people are of two groups:

1. The truthful believer: **"And he (Muhammad (ﷺ)) who has brought the truth and (those who) believed therein."**

2. The lying disbeliever: **"Who utters a lie against Allāh, and denies the truth."**

The truthful believer is the one who comes with truthfulness and believes in it. He is the one whose knowledge and action are both sound. Thus, the correctness of knowledge is [achieved] by believing in the truth and the correctness of deeds is by being truthful. Also, by this, it is known that just as Truthfulness with Allah is a worship of the heart, it is similarly an act that must be manifested in all the limbs. Just as he is required to be truthful from the heart, he is likewise required to be thus with the tongue and limbs. For this reason, similar to how the heart is characterized as being truthful, the tongue and the limbs are characterized as being truthful.

From the descriptions of the tongue as being truthful is what comes in the tremendous supplication in the *Hadīth* of Shadād ibn Aws (رَضِيَاللَّهُعَنْهُ) who said:

قَالَ لِي رَسُولُ الله صَلَّى اللهُ عَلَيْهِ وَ سَلَّمَ : يَا شَدَّادُ بْنَ أَوْسٍ ، إِذَا رَأَيْتَ النَّاسَ قَدِ اكْتَنَزُوا الذَّهَبَ وَ الْفِضَّةَ ، فَاكْنِزْ هَؤُلَاءِ الْكَلِمَاتِ : اللَّهُمَّ إِنِّي أَسْأَلُكَ الثَّبَاتَ فِي الْأَمْرِ ، وَ الْعَزِيمَةَ عَلَى الرُّشْدِ ، وَ أَسْأَلُكَ مُوجِبَاتِ رَحْمَتِكَ ، وَ عَزَائِمَ

مَغْفِرَتِكَ ، وَ أَسْأَلُكَ شُكْرَ نِعْمَتِكَ ، وَ حُسْنَ

عِبَادَتِكَ ، وَ أَسْأَلُكَ قَلْبًا سَلِيمًا ، وَ لِسَانًا

صَادِقًا ، وَ أَسْأَلُكَ مِنْ خَيْرِ مَا تَعْلَمُ ن وَ أَعُوذُ

بِكَ مِنْ شَرِّ مَا تَعْلَمُ ، وَ أَسْتَغْفِرُكَ لِمَا تَعْلَمُ

، إِنَّكَ أَنْتَ عَلَّامُ الْغُيُوبِ .

"The Messenger of Allāh (ﷺ) said to me:

'O Shadād ibn Aws! When you see the people amassing gold and silver, upon you is to amass these statements:

'O Allāh! Verily, I ask you for steadfastness in the affair, determination upon guidance, and I ask You for the causes that bring about your mercy and the resolve for your forgiveness. I ask you for gratefulness for your blessing and excellence on your worship. I ask You for a heart that is intact and for a truthful tongue. I ask You for the good of that which You know, and I seek refuge with You from the evil of that which You know. I seek your forgiveness for that which You know. Verily, You are completely familiar with the matters of the Unseen.'"[10]

He (ﷺ) said: "**A truthful tongue,**" and the truthful tongue is that which agrees with the heart so that the hidden and the apparent are equal: the tongue and the heart are equal. A truthful tongue is not that an individual says with his tongue that which he does believe in his heart.

With regards to the mentioning of this great supplication, within it is a safeguard for the servant, especially when the hearts turn their attention towards this worldly life and are tried by it; and the Prophet (ﷺ) directed attention to this tremendous supplication in such an instance. He said: "**When you see the people amassing gold and silver,**" meaning, when their hearts are turned to this worldly life and are tried by it, and it becomes their greatest concern, the extent of their knowledge and the preoccupation that busies them; then amass these supplications.

---

[10] Reported by at-Tabarānī in 'al-Mu'jam al-Kabīr (7135), and in ad-Du'ā' (631), and Abū Nu'aym in al-Hilyah (1/265).

In fact, if you ponder over the contents of these supplications and what they contain of elevated requests and lofty meanings, you will find that within it is salvation for the servant; and the explanation for this is lengthy.

As for characterizing the limbs with truthfulness or lying, it is in an authentic *Hadīth* where the Prophet (صَلَّىٰاللَّهُعَلَيْهِوَسَلَّمَ) said:

كُتِبَ عَلَى ابْنِ آدَمَ نَصِيبُهُ مِنَ الزِّنَا ، مُدْرِكٌ ذَلِكَ لَا مَحَالَةَ ، فَالْعَيْنَانِ زِنَاهُمَا النَّظَرُ ، وَ الْأُذْنَانِ زِنَاهُمَا الْاسْتِمَاعُ ، وَ اللِّسَانُ زِنَاهُ الْكَلَامُ ، وَ الْيَدُ زِنَاهَا الْبَطْشُ ، وَ الرِّجْلُ زِنَاهَا الْخُطَا ، وَ الْقَلْبُ يَهْوَى وَ يَتَمَنَّى ، وَ يُصَدِّقُ ذَلِكَ الْفَرْجُ وَ يُكَذِّبُهُ .

"Allāh has written the very portion of fornication that a man will indulge in. There will be no escape from it. The fornication of the eye is the (lustful) look, the fornication of the ears is the listening (to voluptuous songs

or talk), the fornication of the tongue is (the licentious) speech, the fornication of the hand is the (lustful) grip, the fornication of the feet is the walking (to the place where he intends to commit fornication), the heart yearns and desires, and the private parts approve all that or disapprove it."[11] [12]

The description of the action of the limbs with truthfulness and lying is the Prophet's (ﷺ) statement: **"And the private parts approve all that or disapprove it."** For this reason, actions themselves are divided into two categories: truthful actions and untruthful actions.

When it is said: "Verily, truthfulness is a safeguard," the meaning of that is that safety for the servant lies in having truthfulness in the heart as a belief, a statement of the tongue, and action of the limbs. It is compulsory that all of this is truthful.

Contemplate the meaning of the verse known as the people of knowledge as the verse of *Birr* (Piety):

---

[11] Reported by al-Bukhārī (6243), Muslim (2657) and it is his wording from the Hadīth of Abū Hurayrah (رضي الله عنه).

﴿ ۞ لَّيْسَ ٱلْبِرَّ أَن تُوَلُّواْ وُجُوهَكُمْ قِبَلَ ٱلْمَشْرِقِ وَٱلْمَغْرِبِ وَلَٰكِنَّ ٱلْبِرَّ مَنْ ءَامَنَ بِٱللَّهِ وَٱلْيَوْمِ ٱلْأَخِرِ وَٱلْمَلَٰٓئِكَةِ وَٱلْكِتَٰبِ وَٱلنَّبِيِّۧنَ وَءَاتَى ٱلْمَالَ عَلَىٰ حُبِّهِۦ ذَوِى ٱلْقُرْبَىٰ وَٱلْيَتَٰمَىٰ وَٱلْمَسَٰكِينَ وَٱبْنَ ٱلسَّبِيلِ وَٱلسَّآئِلِينَ وَفِى ٱلرِّقَابِ وَأَقَامَ ٱلصَّلَوٰةَ وَءَاتَى ٱلزَّكَوٰةَ وَٱلْمُوفُونَ بِعَهْدِهِمْ إِذَا عَٰهَدُواْ وَٱلصَّٰبِرِينَ فِى ٱلْبَأْسَآءِ وَٱلضَّرَّآءِ وَحِينَ ٱلْبَأْسِ أُوْلَٰٓئِكَ ٱلَّذِينَ صَدَقُواْ وَأُوْلَٰٓئِكَ هُمُ ٱلْمُتَّقُونَ ۝ ﴾

"It is not al-Birr (piety, righteousness, and each and every act of obedience to Allāh, etc.) that you turn your faces towards east and (or) west (in prayers); but al-Birr is (the quality of) the one who believes in Allāh, the Last Day, the Angels, the Book, the Prophets and gives his wealth, in spite of love for it, to the kinsfolk, to the orphans, and to al-Masākīn (the poor), and to the wayfarer, and to those who ask, and to set slaves free, performs as-

Salāt (Iqāmat-as-Salāt), and gives the Zakāt, and who fulfill their covenant when they make it, and who are patient in extreme poverty and ailment (disease) and at the time of fighting (during the battles). Such are the people of the truth, and they are al-Muttaqūn (the pious)." [*Sūrah al-Baqarah* 2:177]

The statement of Allāh (*Jalla fe 'ulāh),* in its conclusion: **"Such are the people of the truth,"** returns to two matters:

1. The correct belief. And it is by way of the correctness of their hearts with the foundations of *Imān:* **"but al-Birr is (the quality of) the one who believes in Allāh, the Last Day, the Angels, the Book, the Prophets."** These are the foundations of *Imān;* which it is established; they are for the religion as are the foundations for the trees and building structures.

﴿ أَلَمۡ تَرَ كَيۡفَ ضَرَبَ ٱللَّهُ مَثَلًا كَلِمَةً طَيِّبَةً كَشَجَرَةٖ طَيِّبَةٍ أَصۡلُهَا ثَابِتٞ وَفَرۡعُهَا فِى ٱلسَّمَآءِ ٢٤ ﴾

"See you not how Allāh sets forth a parable? A goodly word as a goodly tree, whose root is firmly fixed, and its branches (reach) to the sky." [*Sūrah Ibrāhīm* 14:24]

Therefore, just as the tree has a foundation with which it cannot be established except upon it, *Imān* has foundations with which it cannot be established except upon them. And the place for the foundations of *Imān* is the heart as mentioned here: **"but al-Birr is (the quality of) the one who believes in Allāh, the Last Day, the Angels, the Book, and the Prophets:"** having *Imān* in Allāh as The Lord and Creator, having *Imān* in His Most Beautiful Names and Lofty Attributes, and having *Imān* that He is the One Who is worshipped in truth and none is worshipped in truth other than Him; and also singling Him out alone with worship, and having sincerity in the religion for Him alone and freeing oneself from Shirk and its people; having *Imān* in the Angels — that great army — their names, descriptions, numbers and assignments generally in what has been made general and in detail what has been made elaborated just as Allāh (عَزَّوَجَلَّ) has ordered with and has come in the *Sunnah* of the Messenger of Allāh (صَلَّى ٱللَّهُ عَلَيْهِ وَسَلَّمَ).

Also, from the foundations is having *Imān* in the Books, meaning every book that Allāh (عَزَّوَجَلَّ) has sent down to every Messenger:

﴿ فَلِذَٰلِكَ فَٱدْعُ وَٱسْتَقِمْ كَمَا أُمِرْتَ وَلَا تَتَّبِعْ أَهْوَآءَهُمْ وَقُلْ ءَامَنتُ بِمَآ أَنزَلَ ٱللَّهُ مِن كِتَٰبٍ وَأُمِرْتُ لِأَعْدِلَ بَيْنَكُمُ ٱللَّهُ رَبُّنَا وَرَبُّكُمْ لَنَآ أَعْمَٰلُنَا وَلَكُمْ أَعْمَٰلُكُمْ لَا حُجَّةَ بَيْنَنَا وَبَيْنَكُمُ ٱللَّهُ يَجْمَعُ بَيْنَنَا وَإِلَيْهِ ٱلْمَصِيرُ ۝ ﴾

"So to this (religion of Islām alone and this Qur'ān) then invite (people) (O Muhammad [صَلَّى ٱللَّهُ عَلَيْهِ وَسَلَّمَ]), and stand firm (on Islâmic Monotheism) as you are commanded, and follow not their desires but say: "I believe in whatsoever Allāh has sent down of the Book [all the holy Books, – this Qur'ān and the Books of the old from the Taurāt (Torah), or the Injīl (Gospel) or the Pages of Ibrāhīm (Abraham)] and I am commanded to do justice among you. Allāh is our Lord and your Lord.

For us our deeds and for you your deeds. There is no dispute between you and us. Allāh will assemble us (all), and to Him is the final return." [*Sūrah ash-Shūrā* 42:15]

Moreover, having *Imān* that He sent them down as guidance to all of the creation and as salvation for the servants, and what they contain of the truth and guidance and that whoever has believed in them will be successful and happy and whoever has disbelieved in them unsuccessful and a loser.

And to similarly have *Imān* in the Prophets, those whom Allāh (سُبْحَانَهُوَتَعَالَ) has sent as givers of glad tidings and warners; to believe in and attest to the truthfulness of every Messenger that Allāh (عَزَّوَجَلَّ) has sent and that they conveyed the clear message and did not leave any good except they directed their nation to it and no evil except they warned their nation from it; and to have *Imān* in the Last Day, the Promised Day, the Day of reward and recompense and it includes everything that occurs after death; and to have *Imān* in the details related to that coming Day from the Book and *Sunnah*. All of these aspects of belief, their place is in the heart.

2. The correctness of actions and that is with good compliance and submission to Allāh (تَبَارَكَوَتَعَالَى) by fulfilling what He legislated and were far from what Allāh (تَبَارَكَوَتَعَالَى) has forbidden us from. All of this is from having truthfulness with Allāh (جَلَّوَعَلَا).

For this reason, establishment of the *Salāh*, givingZakāh, and fulfillment of the Islamic obligations which the servant has been ordered with is from the signs of truthfulness with Allāh (جَلَّوَعَلَا). The signs of truthfulness are not that his circumstance in worship and executing the obligations is a selective condition. In such a manner that he does from the obligations what his self is interested in and what his self is not interested in he leaves off from doing! This is not from the signs of those who are truthful with Allāh.

Thus from this, it is apparent that truthfulness with Allāh is in knowledge, action, belief, and legislation. Truthfulness with Allāh is not something that is in the heart and does not have an effect on the limbs of the servant; rather, truthfulness with Allāh (جَلَّوَعَلَا) is the soundness of what is hidden and what is apparent, in secret and in public as clarified by the statement of our Noble Prophet (ﷺ):

$$
أَلَا وَ إِنَّ فِي الْجَسَدِ مُضْغَةً ، إِذَا صَلَحَتْ صَلَحَ الْجَسَدُ كُلُّهُ ، وَ إِذَا فَسَدَتْ فَسَدَ الْجَسَدُ كُلُّهُ ، أَلَا وَ هِيَ الْقَلْبُ.
$$

"Verily, in the body there is a morsel of flesh if it is correct the rest of the body is correct and if it is corrupt the rest of the body is corrupt. Indeed, it is the heart."[13]

Within this is a clarification that the correctness of the heart along with having truthfulness with Allāh (تَبَارَكَوَتَعَالَى) reflects on the tongue of a man making it a truthful tongue; and also upon the limbs of the servant making them truthful in their establishment of Allāh's obedience.

Also, it is understood from the previous verse (i.e., *Sūrah ash-Shūrā* 42:15) that the actions of the limbs and the apparent legislations of *Islām*; they are all

---

[13] Reported by al-Bukhārī (52), and Muslim (1599) from the Hadīth of Nuʿmān Ibn Bashīr (رَضِيَاللَّهُعَنْهُ)

manifestations of truthfulness with Allāh if they originate from the heart of a sincere individual. For this reason—as an example—contemplate over what has been reported by 'Abdullāh Ibn 'Amr (رَضِيَاللَّهُعَنْهُمَا) from the Prophet (صَلَّىاللَّهُعَلَيْهِوَسَلَّمَ) who mentioned the *Salāh* one day, saying:

مَنْ حَافَظَ عَلَيْهَا كَانَتْ لَهُ نُورًا ، وَ بُرْهَانًا ، وَ

نَجَاةً يَوْمَ الْقِيَامَةِ ، وَ مَنْ لَمْ يُحَافِظْ عَلَيْهَا

لَمْ يَكُنْ لَهُ نُورٌ، وَ لَا بُرْهَانٌ، وَ لَا نَجَاةٌ ، وَ كَانَ

يَوْمَ الْقِيَامَةِ مَعَ قَارُونَ ، وَ فِرْعَوْنَ، وَ هَامَانَ، وَ

أُبَيِّ بْنِ خَلَفٍ .

"Whoever preserves them, there will be for him a light, an evidence, and safety on the Day of Standing. And whoever does not preserve them, there will be no light nor evidence, nor safety for him. And on the Day of Standing he

will be with Qārun, Fir'aun, Hāmān, and Ubay
Ibn Khalaf."[14]

These four individuals are the leaders of disbelief and
its pillars. And this Ubay Ibn Khalaf is an individual
from amongst the *Mushrikūn* (polytheists) to whom the
Prophet (ﷺ) gave the glad tiding that he was
going to kill him with his hand, and he did not kill
anyone before or after him. The proof from this *Hadīth*
is his statement: **"Whoever preserves them it will be
for him a light, an evidence, and safety."** His
statement: **"an evidence,"** means for the truthfulness
of his *Imān*. Another narration similar to this is the
statement of the Prophet (ﷺ):

وَ الـصَّـدَقَـةُ بُـرْهَـانٌ

"And *Sadaqah* (charity) is an evidence."[15]

The *Salāh* is one of the obligations of *Islām and* a pillar
from amongst its great pillars. It is named *Salāh*
because it is the connection between the servant and

---

[14] Reported by Ahmad in '*al-Musnad*' (6576), ad-Dārimī in his
'*Sunnan*' (2763), and at-Tabarānī in '*al-Mu'jam al-Kabīr*' (163,
14746).
[15] Reported by Muslim (223) from the Hadīth of Abū Mālik al-
Ash'arī (﵁) Malik al-Ash'arī (﵁)

Allāh (عَزَّوَجَلَّ). So whoever abandons the *Salāh* has cut the connection, and whoever neglects the *Salāh* is even more neglectful concerning other matters. And If you ponder over the sending down of the obligations upon our Prophet (صَلَّى ٱللَّهُ عَلَيْهِ وَسَلَّمَ), you will find that the first of what was obligated upon the Prophet (صَلَّى ٱللَّهُ عَلَيْهِ وَسَلَّمَ) is *Tawhīd*; for verily, the verses with which he was sent with and through which he became a Messenger is the statement of Allāh (سُبْحَانَهُ وَتَعَالَى):

يَٰٓأَيُّهَا ٱلۡمُدَّثِّرُ ۝ قُمۡ فَأَنذِرۡ ۝ وَرَبَّكَ فَكَبِّرۡ ۝ وَثِيَابَكَ فَطَهِّرۡ ۝ وَٱلرُّجۡزَ فَٱهۡجُرۡ ۝

"O you (Muhammad [صَلَّى ٱللَّهُ عَلَيۡهِ وَسَلَّمَ]) enveloped in garments! Arise and warn! And magnify your Lord (Allāh)! And purify your garments! And keep away from *ar-Rujz* (the idols)!" [*Sūrah al-Muddhittir* 74:1-5]

Thus, he ordered with *Tawhīd* and sincerity and staying away from Shirk. He carried out the call to *Tawhīd* for ten complete years in which no other obligation was revealed to him other than it. After he completed the entire ten years (عَلَيۡهِ ٱلصَّلَاةُ وَٱلسَّلَامُ), he was made to ascend the Seven Heavens and thus the *Salāh* was obligated upon him as fifty prayers after which it was ultimately lightened to five prayers to be performed in the day and night. Hence, the five *Salāh* performed came to equal the fifty in reward.

The matter remained in this state until he migrated to Madinah and after residing there for two years, fasting and *Zakāh* were obligated upon him. Then five years went by and in the ninth year after the migration, *Hajj* (Pilgrimage) was obligated. On top of this, you see some who make Hajj but don't pray?! Do they understand *Islām*?!

On the contrary, you see he who makes *Hajj* and comes with that which nullifies *Tawhīd* and destroys the Religion by turning to other than Allāh (جَلَّوَعَلَا) in supplication. During his *Hajj*, he asks for help from other than Allāh; he resorts to other than Allāh to appeal for aid; he requests cure and rectification of his affairs from other than Allāh; So, has he established the Religion for Allāh (سُبْحَانَهُوَتَعَالَى) as he was ordered?! Has he actualized truthfulness in his servitude to Allāh (جَلَّوَعَلَا) by being sincere in his deeds to Allāh (جَلَّوَعَلَا) and truthful in following the Messenger of Allāh (صَلَّىٰ ٱللَّهُ عَلَيْهِ وَسَلَّمَ)?!

For this reason, truthfulness with Allāh (تَبَارَكَ وَتَعَالَىٰ) is salvation for the servant in his heart with *Tawhīd*, *Imān*, sincerity, submissiveness, and love for Allāh (تَبَارَكَ وَتَعَالَىٰ) and also obedience and compliance to His command.

If the servant's truthfulness with Allāh (تَبَارَكَ وَتَعَالَىٰ) is correct and his heart is truthful with Allāh (تَبَارَكَ وَتَعَالَىٰ), the limbs will be upright as a result of the uprightness of the heart—that is inevitable, since the limbs cannot avoid what the heart desires. The corruption from the limbs, whether the tongue or the other body parts return to the corruption within the heart and a flaw in it and weakness in its truthfulness with Allāh (تَبَارَكَ وَتَعَالَىٰ) and drawing near to Him (جَلَّ وَعَلَا).

All of this is from the matters that emphasize the importance of truthfulness with Allāh, the magnitude of its nature, and how it is mandatory upon the servant to be truthful with Allāh (تَبَارَكَ وَتَعَالَىٰ) and not let the trials and tribulations of the worldly life, its amusements, and its many distractions seize him: if people are afflicted by these matters, they turn them away from the path of truthfulness with Allāh (تَبَارَكَ وَتَعَالَىٰ) and turn them towards the crooked and deviated paths that lead to destruction which they might consider at first to be beauty, adornment, and good that he will acquire; while behold, it is like a mirage that the thirsty considers to be water until he comes to it and does not find anything. So all of it misguides the person away from truthfulness with Allāh (تَبَارَكَوَتَعَالَى) and turns him to many deviant paths away from Allāh's straight path.

This meaning has occurred in the *Hadīth* that has been reported by Imām Ahmad in *al-Musnad* and other than him on the authority of an-Nawās Ibn Sam'ān al-Ansārī (رَضِيَٱللَّهُعَنْهُ) that the Prophet (صَلَّىٱللَّهُعَلَيْهِوَسَلَّمَ) said:

ضَرَبَ اللهُ مَثَلاً صِرَاطًا مُسْتَقِيماً ، وَ عَلَى

جَنْبَتَيْ الصِّرَاطِ سُورَانِ فِيهِمَا أَبْوَابٌ مُفَتَّحَةٌ ،

وَ عَلَى الْأَبْوَابِ سُتُورٌ مُرْخَاةٌ ، وَ عَلَى بَابِ

الصِّرَاطِ دَاعٍ يَقُولُ: أَيُّهَا النَّاسُ ادْخُلُوا الصِّرَاطَ

جَمِيعًا ، وَ لَا تَتَعَرَّجُوا، وَ دَاعٍ يَدْعُو مِنْ فَوْقِ

الصِّرَاطِ ، فَإِذَا أَرَادَ يَفْتَحُ شَيْئًا مِنْ تِلْكَ الْأَبْوَابِ

، قَالَ : وَيْحَكَ لَا تَفْتَحْهُ ، فَإِنَّكَ إِنْ تَفْتَحْهُ

تَلِجْهُ ، وَ الصِّرَاطُ الْإِسْلَامُ ، وَ السُّورَانِ : حُدُودُ اللهِ

، وَ الْأَبْوَابُ الْمُفَتَّحَةُ : مَحَارِمُ اللهِ ، وَ ذَلِكَ الدَّاعِي

عَلَى رَأْسِ الصِّرَاطِ : كِتَابُ اللهِ ، وَ الدَّاعِي مِنْ فَوْقَ

الصِّرَاطِ : وَاعِظُ اللهِ فِي قَلْبِ كُلِّ مُسْلِمٍ .

"Indeed Allāh has made a parable of the straight path: At the two sides of the path there are two walls in which are open doors, each door having a soft curtain. There is a caller at the head of the path calling: "O people! Enter the path all together and do not zigzag", and a caller calling from above the path. If he wants to open something from those doors, the caller will say: "Woe unto you! Do not open it; for if you open it, you will surely enter it." The path is Islām. The walls are the *Hudūd* (legal limitations) of Allāh. The open doors are the prohibitions of Allāh. That caller at the head of the path is the Book of Allāh (i.e. the Qur'ān). The caller above the path is Allāh's exhortation that is in the heart of every Muslim."[16]

This great example clarifies for us the criterion for this issue; and it becomes evident through this, the extent of his truthfulness in his course upon this path and his adhering to it; or it may be that he will not be successful in this test as has proceeded in the noble verse:

$$﴿ وَلَقَدْ فَتَنَّا ٱلَّذِينَ مِن قَبْلِهِمْ ۖ فَلَيَعْلَمَنَّ ٱللَّهُ ٱلَّذِينَ صَدَقُوا۟ وَلَيَعْلَمَنَّ ٱلْكَٰذِبِينَ ٣ ﴾$$

"And We indeed tested those who were before them. And Allāh will certainly make (it) known (the truth of) those who are true, and will certainly make (it) known (the falsehood of) those who are liars, (although Allāh knows all that before putting them to test." [*Sūrah al-Ankabut* 29:3]

One who is on a journey to Allāh (عَزَّوَجَلَّ) and to the obtainment of His Pleasure (سُبْحَانَهُۥوَتَعَالَىٰ) is the same as a

---

[16] Reported by Ahmad in *al-Musnad* (17634) and this is his wording, *at-Tirmidhī* in his *al-Jāmi'* (2859), an-Nisā'ī in *Sunan al-Kubrā'* (11169), and al-Hākim in *al-Mustadrak* (245).

47 | P a g e

man who travels upon a straight path. If he proceeds upon the course without deviating, then that is indicative of his truthfulness, and he will obtain Allāh's pleasure (تَبَارَكَوَتَعَالَ) and the *Jannah* (Paradise). On the two sides of this path are soft-curtained doors, doors that not known to have any locks, so they do not require time or work to open them. And the doors that misguide the people from the path of truthfulness with Allāh are many.

So the matter requires that the servant struggle against his soul while seeking assistance from the Lord (جَلَّوَعَلَا). Allāh (عَزَّوَجَلَّ) said:

﴿ وَٱلَّذِينَ جَٰهَدُواْ فِينَا لَنَهْدِيَنَّهُمْ سُبُلَنَا ۚ وَإِنَّ ٱللَّهَ لَمَعَ ٱلْمُحْسِنِينَ ۝ ﴾

"As for those who strive hard in Us (Our Cause), We will surely guide them to Our Paths. And verily, Allāh is with the Muhsinīn (good-doers)." [*Sūrah al-Ankabut* 29:69]

And the Prophet (صَلَّىٰاللَّهُعَلَيْهِوَسَلَّمَ) said:

احْرِصْ عَلَى مَا يَنْفَعُكَ ، وَاسْتَعِنْ بِاللهِ ، وَ لَا

تَعْجَزْ

"Aspire for what will benefit you and seek
assistance in Allāh and do not be incapable."[17]

There is a subtle point that is befitting to mention in
this context: *Sidq* (truthfulness) has appeared in the
Qur'ān annexed with five things:

1. The entry of *Sidq*
2. The exit of *Sidq*
3. The reward of *Sidq*
4. The honorable mention (*Sidq*)
5. The seat of *Sidq*

1-2. As for the entry and exit of *Sidq*, it is in the
statement of Allāh (تَبَارَكَ وَتَعَالَى):

﴿ وَقُل رَّبِّ أَدْخِلْنِي مُدْخَلَ صِدْقٍ وَأَخْرِجْنِي مُخْرَجَ صِدْقٍ
وَٱجْعَل لِّي مِن لَّدُنكَ سُلْطَٰنًا نَّصِيرًا ۝ ﴾

"And say My Lord! Let my entry (to the city of al-Madinah) be *Sidq* (good), and (likewise) my exit (from the city of Makkah) be *Sidq* (good)." [*Sūrah al-Isra* 17:80]

3. As for the reward of *Sidq*, it is in the statement of Allāh (تَبَارَكَ وَتَعَالَى):

$$﴿ وَبَشِّرِ ٱلَّذِينَ ءَامَنُوٓاْ أَنَّ لَهُمۡ قَدَمَ صِدۡقٍ عِندَ رَبِّهِمۡ ﴾$$

"And give good news to those who believe (in the Oneness of Allāh and His Prophet Muhammad [صَلَّى ٱللَّهُ عَلَيۡهِ وَسَلَّمَ]) that they shall have with their Lord the rewards of their good deeds." [*Sūrah Yūnus* 10:2]

4. As for the honorable mention (*Sidq*), it is in the statement of Allāh (تَبَارَكَ وَتَعَالَى):

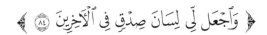

$$﴿ وَٱجۡعَل لِّي لِسَانَ صِدۡقٍ فِي ٱلۡأٓخِرِينَ ٨٤ ﴾$$

"And grant me an honorable mention in later generations." [*Sūrah ash-Shu'rā* 26:84]

5. And as for the seat of *Sidq*, it is in the statement of Allāh the Most-High:

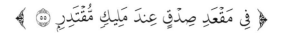

"In a seat of truth (i.e. Paradise), near the Omnipotent King (Allāh, the One, the All-Blessed, the Most High, the Owner of Majesty and Honor)." [*Sūrah al-Qamar* 54:55]

These five matters above that are mentioned in the Qur'ān and are attributed to *Sidq, in fact,* are inseparable and linked to each other. It is like a valuable necklace, of which some of its beads connect to others and lead to each other. It begins with the entry and exit of *Sidq* so that the servant's movements and wanderings, his entry and exit, his going and returning be for Allāh's sake and in agreement with His command. If the servant executes this, he would certainly set forth for himself a tremendous matter that will be safety for him the Day he meets Allāh, and it is the reward of *Sidq*. From the best interpretations of the meaning of, **"Rewards of their good deeds,"** is that it means righteous actions that Allāh (سُبْحَانَهُوَتَعَالَى) grants a person the success to perform in this life:

"And send (good deeds, or ask Allāh to bestow upon you pious offspring) for your own selves beforehand." [*Sūrah al-Baqarah* 2:223]

Because, one's existence in this world is an opportunity for him to send forth goodness that he will find with Allāh on the Day of Resurrection.

And this truthfulness gives fruit to an honorable mention of an individual amongst the people, a pleasant praise and acknowledgment of his achievements and virtues.

For how many people that Allāh has caused to die from ancient generations and through the passing of days and nights are still mentioned by the people: praising, and benefitting from them along with mentioning them with what is beautiful. The Companions (رَضِيَاللَّهُعَنْهُم) have the most abundant portion and greatest share of that. This is from the hastened glad tidings that come in this life; as for the Hereafter, they will have a seat of truth (i.e. Paradise) near Allāh:

$$﴿ فِي مَقْعَدِ صِدْقٍ عِندَ مَلِيكٍ مُّقْتَدِرٍ ۝ ﴾$$

"In a seat of truth (i.e. Paradise), near the Omnipotent King (Allāh, the One, the All-Blessed, the Most-High, the Owner of Majesty and Honor)." [*Sūrah al-Qamar* 54:55]

He connected these five that have been linked with *Sidq* (truthfulness) to each other; every one of them leading to the other and bringing it into effect. And Success is in the Hand of Allāh alone with no partners; He alone is the helper and the One, Who gives success to whomever He wills from His servants in having *Sidq* with Him. And there is no power nor might except with Allāh.

Also [it should be known that] indeed, from the signs of truthfulness with Allāh (تَبَارَكَوَتَعَالَى) is that a person's greatest concern is the Hereafter; and what is not from the signs of truthfulness with Allāh is that a person makes his greatest concern the life of this world to the extent that he only gives the Hereafter what is left over from his time. In the supplication reported from our Prophet (ﷺ), he said:

وَ لَا تَجْعَلِ الـدُّنْيَا أَكْبَرَ هَـمِّنَا ، وَ لَا مَبْلَغَ عِلْمِنَا.

"[O Allāh] do not make this worldly life our greatest concern or the extent of our knowledge."[18]

When asked about intricacies and details of worldly matters, you will find that some people are proficient concerning it to the highest extent; however, if you ask such a person about the commandments for whose sake he was created and for whose fulfillment he was brought into existence, he does not know them. Allāh said describing the disbelievers:

﴿ يَعْلَمُونَ ظَاهِرًا مِّنَ الْحَيَوٰةِ الدُّنْيَا وَهُمْ عَنِ الْآخِرَةِ هُمْ غَافِلُونَ ٧ ﴾

---

[18] Reported by at-Tirmidhī in his *Jāmi'* (3502), an-Nasā'ī in *'Aml al-Yawml- wal Laylah* (446), and al-Bazāra in *'al-Musnad* (5989)

"They know only the outside appearance of the life of this world (i.e. the matters of their livelihood, like irrigating or sowing or reaping), and they are heedless of the Hereafter." [*Sūrah ar-Rūm* 30:7]

Where is the truthfulness with Allāh when the condition of a person in this world is that he does not know the obligations for what he had been created for?

It has preceded that the actualization of truthfulness with Allāh (تَبَارَكَوَتَعَالَ) is only by way of having knowledge of the 'Aqīdah (creed), legislation, obedience, compliance, and submission to Allāh. Verily, the more a person increases in knowledge about his religion and acts according to it he will increase in truthfulness.

On account of this, the highest degree in the religion is truthfulness. It is the degree that follows the one of the Prophets:

﴿ وَمَن يُطِعِ ٱللَّهَ وَٱلرَّسُولَ فَأُوْلَٰٓئِكَ مَعَ ٱلَّذِينَ أَنْعَمَ ٱللَّهُ

عَلَيْهِم مِّنَ ٱلنَّبِيِّـۧنَ وَٱلصِّدِّيقِينَ وَٱلشُّهَدَآءِ وَٱلصَّٰلِحِينَ

وَحَسُنَ أُوْلَٰٓئِكَ رَفِيقًا ۝ ﴾

"And whoso obeys Allāh and the Messenger (Muhammad (ﷺ)), then they will be in the company of those on whom Allāh has bestowed His Grace, of the Prophets, the truthful, the martyrs, and the righteous. And how excellent these companions are!" [*Sūrah an-Nisā* 4:69]

The best of this nation is Abū Bakr as-Sidīq (رضي الله عنه) who become famous for this great characteristic (i.e., truthfulness). He is also the most virtuous of all of the people after the Prophets. He is not the most virtuous in only the nation of Muhammad (ﷺ); rather, he is the most virtuous of the people from all the nations after the Prophets. There is no one from the nations of the Prophets better than Abū Bakr as-Sidīq, hence the Prophet (ﷺ) said in the authentic *Hadīth*:

أَبُو بَكْرٍ وَ عُمَرُ سَيِّدَا كُهُولِ أَهْلِ الْـجَنَّةِ مِنَ الْأَوَّلِيـنَ وَ الْآخِرِينَ ن مَا خَلَا النَّبِيِّيـنَ وَ الْـمُرْسَلِيـنَ.

"Abū Bakr and 'Umar are the leaders of the mature people of Paradise, the first and the last, except for the Prophets and Messengers."[19]

Here is a glance at the matter of the one who has been forsaken and affiliates himself to this religion while defaming the Sidīq of this nation (رَضِيَاللَّهُعَنْهُ) day and night. Where is the truthfulness with Allāh and where is the reality of piety and *Imān* in Allāh (تَبَارَكَوَتَعَالَى)?! If the worth of the most virtuous and the truthful one of this nation (رَضِيَاللَّهُعَنْهُ) is not known, and is instead defamed with the most severe of defamation with some of the people cursing him in the most severe way; where is the reality of their truthfulness with Allāh while this is their stance against the loftiest of the nations!? Where

---

[19] Reported by at-Tirmidhī (3665, 3666), Ibn Mājah (95), Ahmad (602), and other than them. Shaykh al-Albānī said it is Sahīh in '*as-Sahīhah*' (824)

is the reality of truthfulness if the Sidīq of this nation and their most forward is insulted?!

Truthfulness with Allāh is a matter that was actualized for the noble Companions (رَضِيَٱللَّهُعَنْهُمْ):

﴿ مِّنَ ٱلْمُؤْمِنِينَ رِجَالٌ صَدَقُواْ مَا عَٰهَدُواْ ٱللَّهَ عَلَيْهِ فَمِنْهُم مَّن قَضَىٰ نَحْبَهُ وَمِنْهُم مَّن يَنتَظِرُ وَمَا بَدَّلُواْ تَبْدِيلًا ۝ لِّيَجْزِيَ ٱللَّهُ ٱلصَّٰدِقِينَ بِصِدْقِهِمْ وَيُعَذِّبَ ٱلْمُنَٰفِقِينَ إِن شَآءَ أَوْ يَتُوبَ عَلَيْهِمْ إِنَّ ٱللَّهَ كَانَ غَفُورًا رَّحِيمًا ۝ ﴾

"Among the believers are men who have been true to their covenant with Allāh [i.e. they have gone out for Jihād (holy fighting), and showed not their backs to the disbelievers]; of them some have fulfilled their obligations (i.e. have been martyred); and some of them are still waiting, but they have never changed (i.e. they never proved treacherous to their covenant that they concluded with Allāh) in the least. That Allāh may reward the men of truth for their truth (i.e. for their patience at the accomplishment of that which they covenanted with Allāh), and punish the hypocrites, if He wills, or accept their repentance by turning to them (in Mercy). Verily, Allāh is Ever Oft-Forgiving, Most Merciful." [*Sūrah al-Ahzāb* 33:23-24]

It is sufficient for a person as a virtue, noble trait, and truthfulness with Allāh that his heart is void of ill feelings concerning the Companions (رَضِيَاللهُعَنْهُم) while traversing upon their methodology. Allāh said:

﴿ وَٱلسَّٰبِقُونَ ٱلْأَوَّلُونَ مِنَ ٱلْمُهَٰجِرِينَ وَٱلْأَنصَارِ وَٱلَّذِينَ ٱتَّبَعُوهُم بِإِحْسَٰنٍ ﴾

"And the foremost to embrace Islām of the Muhājirūn (those who migrated from Makkah to al-Madinah) and the Ansār (the citizens of al-Madinah who helped and gave aid to the Muhājirūn) and also those who followed them exactly (in Faith)." [*Sūrah at-Tawbah* 9:100]

Allāh (سُبْحَانَهُوَتَعَالَى) also said:

وَمَن يُشَاقِقِ ٱلرَّسُولَ مِنۢ بَعْدِ مَا تَبَيَّنَ لَهُ ٱلْهُدَىٰ وَيَتَّبِعْ غَيْرَ سَبِيلِ ٱلْمُؤْمِنِينَ نُوَلِّهِۦ مَا تَوَلَّىٰ وَنُصْلِهِۦ جَهَنَّمَ وَسَآءَتْ مَصِيرًا ۝

"And whoever contradicts and opposes the Messenger (Muhammad [ﷺ]) after the right path has been shown clearly to him, and follows other than the believers' way, We shall keep him in the path he has chosen, and burn him in Hell – what an evil destination!" [*Sūrah an-Nisā* 4:115]

In numerous verses of the Qur'ān, Allāh (جَلَّ وَعَلَا) has informed us that He is pleased with them and they with Him. He even praised them in the Taurāt (the Book revealed to Musa (عَلَيْهِ ٱلسَّلَام) and the Injīl (the Book revealed to 'Isā) before they were even created. The Most-High said in the last verse of Sūratul-Fath:

﴿ مُّحَمَّدٌ رَّسُولُ ٱللَّهِ ۚ وَٱلَّذِينَ مَعَهُۥ أَشِدَّآءُ عَلَى ٱلْكُفَّارِ رُحَمَآءُ

بَيْنَهُمْ ۖ تَرَىٰهُمْ رُكَّعًا سُجَّدًا يَبْتَغُونَ فَضْلًا مِّنَ ٱللَّهِ وَرِضْوَٰنًا ۖ

سِيمَاهُمْ فِى وُجُوهِهِم مِّنْ أَثَرِ ٱلسُّجُودِ ۚ ذَٰلِكَ مَثَلُهُمْ فِى ٱلتَّوْرَىٰةِ ۚ

وَمَثَلُهُمْ فِى ٱلْإِنجِيلِ كَزَرْعٍ أَخْرَجَ شَطْـَٔهُۥ فَـَٔازَرَهُۥ فَٱسْتَغْلَظَ

فَٱسْتَوَىٰ عَلَىٰ سُوقِهِۦ يُعْجِبُ ٱلزُّرَّاعَ لِيَغِيظَ بِهِمُ ٱلْكُفَّارَ ۗ وَعَدَ

ٱللَّهُ ٱلَّذِينَ ءَامَنُوا۟ وَعَمِلُوا۟ ٱلصَّٰلِحَٰتِ مِنْهُم مَّغْفِرَةً وَأَجْرًا

عَظِيمًا ٢٩ ﴾

"Muhammad [ﷺ] is the Messenger of Allāh. And those who are with him are severe against disbelievers and merciful among themselves. You see them bowing and falling down prostrate (in prayer), seeking bounty from Allāh and (His) Good Pleasure. The mark of them (i.e. of their Faith) is on their faces (foreheads) from the traces of prostration (during prayers). This is their description in the Taurāt (Torah). However, their description in the Injīl (Gospel) is like a (sown) seed that

sends forth its shoot, then makes it strong, and becomes thick and it stands straight on its stem, delighting the sowers, that He may enrage the disbelievers with them." [*Sūrah al-Fath* 48:29]

This is a beautiful praise from the Lord of all that exists for the Companions before they set foot on earth before they were even created. There are many verses like this in the Qur'ān praising the Companions. So, if someone's heart is afflicted with hatred towards the Companions, he is not truthful with Allāh, nor is he truthful about his *Imān* in the Qur'ān. How can one whose heart is full of hatred for the best of whom Allāh praised in the Qur'ān be truthful in his *Imān* in Allāh and the Qur'ān?!

For this reason, when Allāh praised the Companions, the *Muhājirīn* (those Companions who migrated) and the *Ansār* (those who gave aid to the Muhājirīn) (رَضِيَٱللَّهُعَنْهُمْ) with His statement:

﴿ لِلْفُقَرَاءِ ٱلْمُهَٰجِرِينَ ٱلَّذِينَ أُخْرِجُواْ مِن دِيَٰرِهِمْ وَأَمْوَٰلِهِمْ

يَبْتَغُونَ فَضْلًا مِّنَ ٱللَّهِ وَرِضْوَٰنًا وَيَنصُرُونَ ٱللَّهَ وَرَسُولَهُۥٓ

أُوْلَٰٓئِكَ هُمُ ٱلصَّٰدِقُونَ ٨ ﴾

"(And there is also a share in this booty) for the poor emigrants, who were expelled from their homes and their property, seeking Bounties from Allāh and to please Him, and helping Allāh (i.e. helping His religion – Islamic Monotheism) and His Messenger (Muhammad [ﷺ]). Such are indeed truthful (to what they say)." [*Sūrah al-Hashr* 59:8]

This is a testimony to the truthfulness of the *Muhajirīn* from the Lord of all that exists.

Afterwards, He said about the *Ansār*:

﴿ وَٱلَّذِينَ تَبَوَّءُو ٱلدَّارَ وَٱلْإِيمَٰنَ مِن قَبْلِهِمْ يُحِبُّونَ مَنْ هَاجَرَ

إِلَيْهِمْ وَلَا يَجِدُونَ فِى صُدُورِهِمْ حَاجَةً مِّمَّآ أُوتُواْ وَيُؤْثِرُونَ

عَلَىٰٓ أَنفُسِهِمْ وَلَوْ كَانَ بِهِمْ خَصَاصَةٌ وَمَن يُوقَ شُحَّ نَفْسِهِۦ

فَأُوْلَٰٓئِكَ هُمُ ٱلْمُفْلِحُونَ ٩ ﴾

"And those who, before them, had homes (in Al-Madinah) and had adopted the Faith, love those who emigrate to them, and have no jealousy in their breasts for that which they have been given (from the booty of Banū An-Nadīr), and give them (emigrants) preference over themselves even though they were in need of that. And whosoever is saved from his own covetousness, such are they who will be successful." [*Sūrah al-Hashr* 59:9]

After that He mentioned the condition of the truthful from those who preceded them from the people of truthful *Imān*, He said:

﴿ وَٱلَّذِينَ جَآءُو مِنۢ بَعْدِهِمْ يَقُولُونَ رَبَّنَا ٱغْفِرْ لَنَا

وَلِإِخْوَٰنِنَا ٱلَّذِينَ سَبَقُونَا بِٱلْإِيمَٰنِ وَلَا تَجْعَلْ فِى قُلُوبِنَا

غِلًّا لِّلَّذِينَ ءَامَنُوا۟ رَبَّنَآ إِنَّكَ رَءُوفٌ رَّحِيمٌ ١٠ ﴾

"And those who came after them say: "Our Lord! Forgive us and our brethren who have preceded us in Faith, and put not in our hearts any hatred against those who have believed. Our Lord! You are indeed full of kindness, Most Merciful." [*Sūrah al-Hashr* 59:10]

If there is hatred in the people's heart about those whom Allāh said concerning them: **"Such are indeed the truthful to what they say,"** Indeed, such a people are far from the reality of truthfulness with Allāh (جَلَّوَعَلَا) and belief in His revealed Book and sent Prophet (صَلَّىاللَّهُعَلَيْهِوَسَلَّمَ). Thus whenever the implementation of truthfulness with Allāh is spoken of, it is binding to return to and look at the exalted life, the life of the first group, the Companions of the Prophet (صَلَّىاللَّهُعَلَيْهِوَسَلَّمَ). For indeed, he who has the most resemblance to them is the closest to having truthfulness with Allāh (تَبَارَكَوَتَعَالَى). And whoever is distant from this and has hatred for the Companions of the Prophet (صَلَّىاللَّهُعَلَيْهِوَسَلَّمَ) in his heart, then he has certainly come between himself and the reality of having truthfulness with Allāh (جَلَّوَعَلَا).

Defamation of the Companions is in reality defamation of the religion itself since "defamation of the transmitter is defamation of the transmission." So by this, it is known that insulting the Companions of the Prophet (ﷺ) is a complete disconnection of the people from the actualization of truthfulness with Allāh (جَلَّ وَعَلَا) since the Companions of the Prophet (ﷺ) are the ones who transmitted to us the reality of truthfulness with Allāh (تَبَارَكَ وَتَعَالَى). So if they are slandered, then how would the people actualize truthfulness with Allāh (تَبَارَكَ وَتَعَالَى) while his carriers are insulted?!

Abū Zur'ah ar-Rāzī (رَحِمَهُ ٱللَّه) said:

إِذَا رَأَيْتُمُ الرَّجُلَ يَنْتَقِصُ أَحَدًا مِنْ أَصْحَابِ النَّبِيِّ صَلَّى اللهُ عَلَيْهِ وَ سَلَّمَ فَاعْلَمُوا أَنَّهُ زِنْدِيقٌ ، لِأَنَّ الدِّينَ حَقٌّ ، وَ الْقُرْآنَ حَقٌّ ، وَ إِنَّمَا أَدَّى إِلَيْنَا ذَلِكَ الصَّحَابَة.

"If you see a man belittle anyone from amongst the Companions of the Prophet (ﷺ), know that he is a heretic; because

the religion and the Qur'ān are true and the only ones who conveyed that to us were the Companions."[20]

Reflect here upon the statement of Allāh (عَزَّوَجَلَّ):

﴿ فَلَوْ صَدَقُوا۟ ٱللَّهَ لَكَانَ خَيْرًا لَّهُمْ ۝ ﴾

"Then if they had been true to Allāh, it would have been better for them." [*Sūrah Muhammad* 47:21]

You will see the reality of the benevolence with which you will succeed with Allāh (سُبْحَانَهُوَتَعَالَى) and that it is connected to your truthfulness with Allāh. Whenever you are truthful with Allāh (عَزَّوَجَلَّ), you will succeed with good and there is no success to good except by way of truthfulness with Allāh (عَزَّوَجَلَّ).

And indeed, Allāh has said:

﴿ كُنتُمْ خَيْرَ أُمَّةٍ أُخْرِجَتْ لِلنَّاسِ ﴾

"You are the best people ever raised up for mankind." [*Sūrah Aali Imrān* 3:110]

---

[20] Reported by al-Khatīb al-Baghdādī '*al-'Kifāyah*' (49)

The Companions are the first and foremost to enter into this verse. The Prophet (ﷺ) said:

خَيْرُ النَّاسِ قَرْنِي ، ثُمَّ الَّذِينَ يَلُونَهُمْ ، ثُمَّ الَّذِينَ يَلُونَهُمْ

"The best of people are my generation, and then those who follow after them, then those who follow after them."[21]

That is because the Companions (رَضِيَ اللهُ عَنْهُمْ) — without doubt — actualized this dignity in the best matter and place; and that was good for them. So how great their affair is (رَضِيَ اللهُ عَنْهُمْ)!

This subject matter — as it is not hidden — is a big and vast topic. It is a lofty subject that possesses a great matter. We are all in severe need for having concern and giving importance to it so that safety and success will can be actualized for us the Day we meet Allāh (سُبْحَانَهُ وَتَعَالَى).

---

[21] Reported by al-Bukhārī (2652, 3651), and Muslim (2533) from the Ḥadīth of Ibn Mas'ūd (رَضِيَ اللهُ عَنْهُ)

I ask Allāh, the Most-Generous, the Lord of the Great Throne with His Most Beautiful Names and Most Lofty Attributes to grant us all success to that which He loves and is pleased with from correct statements and righteous actions. And I ask that He rectifies for us our affair, all of it and that He does not entrust us to ourselves for the twinkling of an eye and that He forgives us all; verily, He is the All-Hearer of the supplication, the One we hope in and He is sufficient for the Best Protector and us.

May Allāh send praise and peace upon His slave and Messenger, our Prophet Muhammad, upon his family, and his Companions all-together.

The end of the treatise wal Hamdulillah.

Translation of this treatise has been completed on the 27th night of Ramadhan 1436 Hijri corresponding to July 13th, 2015 in Subkul Ahad- Ashmoon- Al-Munufiyyah- Egypt (may Allāh preserve it) by Abū 'Abdillāh Khalīl 'Abdur-Razzāq.

POINTS OF BENEFIT

POINTS OF BENEFIT

POINTS OF BENEFIT

POINTS OF BENEFIT

Printed in Great Britain
by Amazon